Original title:
A Pocket of Possibilities

Copyright © 2025 Creative Arts Management OÜ
All rights reserved.

Author: Julian Carmichael
ISBN HARDBACK: 978-1-80586-197-3
ISBN PAPERBACK: 978-1-80586-669-5

A Symphony of Untamed Futures

In a world where socks can dance,
The moon wears pajamas by chance.
Pickles may play jazz on a whim,
While cats in tutus dance on a brim.

Bananas hold court with grand flair,
Jellybeans plotting a sticky affair.
Elephants twirl, with flair so bold,
In this chaos, magic unfolds.

Windows to What May Come

Behind each curtain, a chicken may sing,
Riding a bicycle with a monarch's ring.
Potatoes gossip in neon hues,
While cupcakes argue on who's got the blues.

A turtle in a tuxedo applies for a role,
To play in the film of a pancake's stroll.
Rainbows wink from behind the trees,
As trees tickle the clouds with a gentle breeze.

The Alchemy of Ordinary Days

Scrambled eggs debate the latest trend,
While toast applauds for the buttered friend.
Dishes hold meetings in the sink,
Mops dream of walls, as they sip on ink.

Calendars dance on the kitchen floor,
Chasing the vacuum like never before.
The fridge chuckles at expired fate,
As leftovers plan a reunion date.

Journeys within the Fold

In pockets of coats where marbles hide,
A parade of gumdrops takes a ride.
Paperclips form a funky crew,
While secret notes point to the view.

Bicycles dream of flying high,
On trails made of ice cream in the sky.
From crayons' fights to a button's cheer,
Adventure sprouts, oh so near.

Sparked by Serendipity

In a sock, once lost, found gold,
An adventure waiting to be told.
Who knew laundry could spark such fun,
Where mismatched socks dance under the sun?

A daydream caught beneath the bed,
A treasure map that my cat read.
With each little turn, a giggle breaks,
As I navigate this maze of frosted flakes.

A jellybean lurking in my shoe,
Claims to be rainbow, but tastes like glue.
Surprises hide in pockets so deep,
Where laughter echoes, and dreams don't sleep.

The Alchemy of Hope

A pinch of sugar on toast that's burnt,
Transforms my frown, and laughter's churned.
The egg that rolled off the kitchen shelf,
Becomes a chef's hat for my pet elf.

Mixing odd socks with a dash of cheer,
Creating a fashion that's sure to endear.
In the world's quirkiest pantry, I stand,
Stirring the chaos with a shaky hand.

Hope's a recipe made with delight,
Even if dinner ends in a food fight.
With giggles and guffaws, we fill the bowl,
Finding joy in play, that's the ultimate goal.

Inside Every Small Space

Beneath the couch, a mystery waits,
An army of crumbs, my dinner mates.
A circus of dust bunnies takes the stage,
In theaters of fluff, they dance with rage.

A book of secrets in a drawer so tight,
Whispers of wonders in the moonlight.
Each forgotten toy, with tales of yore,
Invites my imagination to explore.

In the smallest corners, adventure hides,
Like where my lost calendar slides.
Celebrating moments, both weird and sweet,
Finding fun where life feels discreet.

Realms Yet to be Discovered

Beneath my bed lies a kingdom vast,
With monsters that laugh and shadows that cast.
An upside-down world, where socks rule the day,
Sending all dust mites packing, hip-hip-hooray!

A refrigerator, portal to the bizarre,
Where leftovers rule and pickles go far.
Unlikely friendships in jars stacked high,
Talking to veggies, I can't tell a lie.

In cabinets dark, where the spices collide,
Uncharted flavors, oh, what a ride!
Inventing recipes with a wink and a grin,
As I deconstruct dinner, let the chaos begin!

Seeds of Wonder in Everyday Life

In the garden of socks, I found a shoe,
Where dreams go to hide, just waiting for you.
A sandwich of jelly, and peanut in play,
Whispers of lunchboxes, brightening the day.

Cats chase their tails with such fervent zeal,
While dogs plot their action, what a grand deal!
In the drawer of left socks, a treasure chest lies,
Filled with oddities, oh how time flies!

Unfolding the Map of Potential

I opened a map, it had crayons and cheese,
A compass of pickles, it's sure to please!
The X marks the spot for the grand pizza pie,
With pepperoni mountains that touch the sky!

In the land of misplaced keys, treasures abound,
You might stumble on laughter, where joy knows no bound.
Each twist of the journey brings giggles in tow,
Adventure awaits where the wild tangents flow!

Kaleidoscope of Untold Stories

In a teacup of quirks, there's magic on brew,
A narrative dances, weaving tales anew.
The spoon is a scribe penning stories of old,
As teabags whisper secrets, like treasures of gold.

With a sprinkle of laughter and a dash of surprise,
Life writes its saga with winks in our eyes.
Every corner holds wonders, a parade of delight,
In the circus of moments, every twist feels just right!

The Canvas of Infinite Choices

On the canvas of chaos, I splash red and green,
With strokes of banana, a colorful scene.
The palette of what-ifs dances with glee,
As my paintbrush explores what could ever be!

Doodles of fortune, twirling in space,
Balloons filled with hopes, a bright, lovely face.
Every line tells a tale, each shade has a voice,
In the gallery of whims, we can freely rejoice!

Glimmers of a Distant Horizon

A cat in a hat, what a sight,
Waving at fish that take flight.
The trees dance a jig, oh so spry,
While squirrels plot worlds from high in the sky.

A ship made of toast sails the sea,
With butter as crew, what a sight to see!
The waves laugh and tickle the mist,
As jellybeans bloom in a candy twist.

Echoes of What Lies Ahead

A frog on a skateboard zooms by,
Chasing a moonbeam that's stuck in the sky.
With helmets made of cheese, they glide,
Through puddles of giggles, they take a wild ride.

The clocks march backward in bright disco shoes,
While ants in tuxedos sing the blues.
In a garden of socks, they hold a grand ball,
Where mismatched live happily, having a ball.

Threads of Time Yet to Weave

Balloons made of jelly float high in the air,
While goldfish recite Shakespeare, without a care.
The whispers of cupcakes start tickling the trees,
And cupcakes giggle back in the teasing breeze.

A rabbit in slippers does breakdancing spins,
While clocks play hide and seek, hoping to win.
With ribbons of laughter and threads made of fun,
The world weaves its magic until the day's done.

In the Cradle of Imagination

A dinosaur in pajamas brews cocoa with flair,
While dreams ride on bicycles through fluffy white air.
The rainbows play hopscotch on clouds up above,
And cupcakes hold court in a castle of love.

A penguin in flip-flops juggles some pies,
While stars wear sunglasses, a trendy disguise.
In fields of confetti and sunshine galore,
The heart of our laughter is what we explore.

Echoes of Future Stars

In a world where socks go missing,
Dreams slip through the night,
Soon they'll dance, perhaps with flair,
Dressing up in neon light.

Who knew a cat could lead the way?
Whiskers pointing to the fun,
Chasing tails amidst the play,
Making shadows on the run.

With pancakes piled to the sky,
And syrup flows like rivers,
Laughing hard, oh me, oh my,
This future's filled with quivers.

So let's ride llamas to the moon,
With hats that spin like dreams,
In this wide world, we'll find our tune,
In funny hats and silly gleams.

Beneath the Surface of Today

Beneath the waves of cluttered clothes,
A treasure map may lie,
With peanut butter on our toes,
And jellyfish that fly.

In the garden, gnomes conspire,
With daffodils in hand,
They scheme for world domination,
Just to form a band.

Watch as ants engage in dance,
With disco balls up high,
While squirrels plot their great advance,
To steal a donut pie.

So let's embrace the silly quirks,
In moments lost in play,
For hidden gems in everyday,
Are waiting—hip hooray!

The Hidden Palette of Life

Life's a canvas with surprise,
Crayons breaking through the night,
With flavors dancing in the skies,
Tasting colors that feel right.

Pickle hats and shoes of cream,
Can we wear them? Yes, indeed!
Walking in a whimsical dream,
Planting spice and spreading seed.

In the pantry, wacky sights,
With sauce that flips and flies,
Tomatoes sing in faint delights,
While lemons squint their eyes.

So let's mix up our potions,
And sip from teacups strange,
Creating wild emotions,
In this wonderful exchange.

Glistening Threads of Destiny

Threads of fate that twist and twirl,
Like spaghetti in a bowl,
As marbles bounce and diamonds swirl,
Chasing laughter makes us whole.

In the closet, shoes take flight,
Socks embark on grand crusades,
They dance beneath the disco light,
In the hall of joyful parades.

With fortune cookies full of quips,
And lemonade that froths,
Our dreams take joyful little trips,
While navigating silly sloths.

So grab your cape and join the fun,
Together we will weave,
With every thread, a new begun,
Life's tapestry to believe.

Tapestry of Unknowns

In the closet, socks collide,
A parade of colors, oh what a ride.
Left and right, they play their tricks,
Like a circus act with no clear fix.

Baking bread, it rises high,
A fluffy cloud that dares to fly.
Yet every time, it makes a mess,
As flour dances, I must confess.

Chasing dreams in tangled sheets,
Dodging hopes on runaway streets.
Each wish a juggler out of tune,
A comedy show beneath the moon.

With every stumble, a new surprise,
Like who knew cheese could wear a disguise?
In this chaos, laughter waits,
A tapestry woven with silly fates.

The Web of Infinite Love

In the garden, bees do waltz,
Dancing round the flowers' faults.
Each buzz, a giggle, sweet and low,
A heart-shaped laugh that starts to grow.

Cats with strategies oh so sly,
Plotting mischief as birds fly by.
Yet every leap is met with grace,
Chasing shadows, a funny race.

Dinner's ready, or so I claim,
But burnt toast steals the spotlight's flame.
With every bite of charred surprise,
Love's laughter echoes, never dies.

In moments shared, that's where it's at,
Finding joy in a cheeky spat.
With every giggle, our hearts align,
In this web, our love's divine.

Glimpses of Tomorrow's Light

The fridge hums a silly tune,
Leftovers plotting, making a swoon.
Each bite could lead to a taste blunder,
Or a culinary love to make you wonder.

Dreams of grandeur in a cereal bowl,
Rehearsing futures, playing a role.
Yet every morning starts the same,
With spoons that giggle, it's all a game.

Chasing rainbows with a hop and a skip,
Every tumble feels like a trip.
With clouds that mimic an ice cream cone,
Laughter bubbles up, we're never alone.

Every whim holds a twinkle bright,
In the absurd, we find delight.
Glimpses burst like fireflies' flight,
Leading us on to tomorrow's light.

Reflections in a Glass of Possibility

Pouring dreams in a fanciful glass,
Each sip a giggle, each laugh a pass.
Reflections dance like silly sprites,
In the murky depths of fun-filled nights.

Watching wishes swirl and twirl,
Like a dance of chaos in a whirl.
With every clink, we toast to the weird,
Here's to the laughter that's always cheered.

Mirrors chuckle when mirrors speak,
Echoing giggles through the cheeky squeak.
Caught in the fun of the playful tease,
Life's a party that aims to please.

So raise your glass to the fun unknown,
In every bubble, the seeds are sown.
Reflections shine with comedic glee,
In this glass, possibilities run free.

The Harmony of Hidden Choices

In a drawer, I found a sock,
A treasure map, just like a rock.
The other pair? Still unknown,
Underneath the couch, all alone.

Mismatched shoes lead the way,
To joyful trips, come what may.
Who needs a plan, let's just roam,
With each wrong turn, we've found a home.

Ruins of Regret and Joys Yet Born

I baked a pie, it flopped and fell,
Tasted like my old gym smell.
Yet laughter filled the kitchen air,
As crumbs flew high without a care.

Regrets are just a path we stroll,
With every misstep, we reach our goal.
Each funny fail, a tale to spin,
From burnt to golden, let's dive in!

Vistas of Wonderment

I wandered through the zoo one day,
To meet a llama, oh, what a play!
It spit at me, but what a sight,
We shared a laugh, both took flight.

The giraffe necked high was quite the tease,
As it stuck its tongue in the trees.
I waved hello, it blinked twice,
It's hard to stay serious with that slice!

Cartography of Curiosity

I drew a map on my arm, you see,
To find the snacks in the kitchen spree.
An X marks the spot where cookies lay,
Where the cat had a very loud say.

Each detour led to a funny face,
The milk spilled out in chaotic grace.
Exploring the depths of my cupboard's lore,
In search of snacks, I found much more!

A Breath of Unfurling Realities

In the bag, I found a shoe,
Mismatched, but who knew?
It may not fit, but that's alright,
I'll dance with joy, not fear the plight.

A half-eaten sandwich greets my glance,
A perfect ticket to a lunch-time dance.
With crumbs as confetti, I twirl around,
Who knew my snacks could be so profound?

A sock with holes, but hey, it's fun,
Maybe it's a puppet for my next pun!
Life's odd treasures bring chuckles wide,
I'll embrace each whimsy, let smiles be my guide.

The Lightness of What Might Be

Imagine if my keys could sing,
Every note a joyous fling.
They rattle and jingle, a tune so bright,
Unlocking laughter, day and night.

A rubber band, a slingshot dream,
Propelling humor in a silly stream.
With every stretch, a joke takes flight,
In this world, all feels just right.

A beach ball stuffed in my coat,
Inflatable joys as I write this note.
Rolling out laughter, soft and round,
Oh, the surprises that can be found!

Treasures in the Everyday

Mushroom hats on heads of dreams,
Kites made of paper, full of gleams.
A spoon began to dance polka,
While the forks played the maraca.

Bounced on a bubble, so carefree,
Chasing the quirks that tickle me.
With mismatched socks as a fashion tease,
I strut my stuff, oh, what a breeze!

A ladder made of wobbly laughs,
Climbing high on silly crafts.
With each step up, the giggles soar,
Every heartbeat begs for more!

Hideaways of Infinite Options

Under the couch, a treasure's found,
Dust bunnies dancing, what a sound!
With every wiggle, they do a jig,
My laughter grows, I'm feeling big.

An umbrella sprouting rainbow dreams,
Catching wishes in shiny beams.
It flips inside out, just like my thoughts,
Tall tales spring forth, like tangled knots.

A keys' ring full of chimes and jests,
Unlocking giggles, it always quests.
In the mundane, I'm a silly king,
Crafting joy from everything!

The Secret Stash of Aspirations

Under my bed lie wild wishes,
A zoo of hopes, all in fine dishes.
They laugh and wiggle, full of glee,
Dreams of dancing on a giant bee.

Each scribble's a secret, each doodle a cheer,
An ice cream mountain, with no one near.
They plan their escape for a sunny day,
When socks turn into boats, and tin cans play.

I find a raccoon, all dressed in style,
He says, "Join us, it'll be worthwhile!"
We'll sail through pancakes, ride clouds in style,
With every giggle, life's a crooked mile.

So here in the chaos, I laugh with flair,
A stash of nonsense, beyond compare.
Who needs a map when you've got a dream?
Let's launch those wishes; watch them beam!

Paths Waiting to Be Walked.

I've got shoes that dance on a whim,
They twirl and twist, ensuring I brim.
Paths are quirky, with mapless fun,
Where squirrels reign under a golden sun.

With each step, a puddle might sing,
A chicken parade or a turtle fling.
Who knew the sidewalk could giggle so loud?
While ants in tuxedos form a proud crowd.

The trees whisper jokes, I swear it's true,
A clever little rabbit whispers too.
He says if you jump, you'll glide like a kite,
And land in a swirl of confetti light.

So let's lace up shoes and take to the street,
Where paths are full of laughter, oh what a treat!
Waltzing with brooms and chatting with frogs,
Life's more delightful with whimsical logs.

Whispers of Untold Dreams

In the corner of my attic high,
There's a stash of dreams that flutter and fly.
With wings of paper, they glide and tease,
Whispers of secrets rustle the leaves.

A chocolate fountain spills tales so sweet,
Of candy-coated worlds with dancing feet.
There's a unicorn dressed as a cat, I swear,
He winks as he munches on licorice hair.

In a sock drawer, a dragon snores,
While marshmallow clouds float through tiny doors.
Each giggle echoes across the night,
As dreams tumble out, taking flight.

So let's gather the whispers, ride the breeze,
Join the parade of socks and candies, please!
For in this realm of dreams we gleam,
Life is a canvas, a silly theme.

Hidden Corners of Hope

In every nook, a giggle sleeps,
Peeking from shadows, in playful heaps.
Under the couch, a hope slips out,
Wearing mismatched socks, twirling about.

Behind the curtains, a starfish sings,
Of seaweed caves and vibrant flings.
Where jellybeans rain on a sunny day,
And gummy worms wiggle without delay.

A teapot grins, sharing its dreams,
Of far-off lands and magical beams.
Each brew bubbles with tales to unfold,
Of socks stuffed with wishes and stories bold.

So let's explore these corners quite merry,
Where hope hops giggling, without a worry.
With laughter and whimsy, let's carry the load,
In hidden corners, joy's waiting to explode!

Cracks of Wonder in the Routine

Each morning I pour my cereal,
It dances like a ballerina in a bowl.
The milk joins in, a frothy whirl,
As spoons rejoice in a rhythmic stroll.

Time ticks slow like a lazy snail,
My sock has gone missing, oh what a tale!
A shoelace speaks of grand escape,
While toast insists, 'I'm not your fate!'

The clock's hands play hide and seek,
As bills sneak in; it's all too bleak.
Yet laughter bubbles, a fizzy delight,
In the cracks of this wondrous sight.

So let's embrace this daily grind,
With silly talks and jokes entwined.
For in the chaos, the fun shall yield,
A world where whimsy is revealed.

The Singularity of Choice

I ponder my lunch on a Tuesday fine,
Peanut butter or jelly — they intertwine.
Do I risk a sandwich explosion today?
Or just delight in crumbs that stray?

The ice cream whistle sings from the stand,
But my wallet replies, 'You're in No Man's Land!'
An option of two, or is it just one?
The universe waits while I toy with fun.

Beneath the mass of decisions galore,
A cookie whispers, 'What's life in store?'
While salads shout 'Green is the way!'
I'm buried in choices that lead me astray.

In this paradox, laughter will bloom,
As I chase the flavors that fight for my room.
With each bite a giggle, each sip a cheer,
The singularity of choice is the best time of year!

Hidden Springs of Hope

In the backyard, a garden of dreams,
Where radishes gossip and lettuce beams.
The weeds think they're plants in a grand charade,
While insects host parties, completely unafraid.

A dandelion winks, 'I'm more than a pest!'
It sprinkles the air with seeds at its best.
While clouds drift lazily, completely bemused,
At the universe's antics, all bright and confused.

Hope springs eternal from these little blooms,
Like a cat in a box, defying life's dooms.
A tumble of petals like laughter in flight,
In nature's own comedy, everything's bright.

So let's plant some dreams on this whimsical plot,
With each sprout, we'll laugh at the troubles we've got.
For in every garden of quirks so divine,
Lies hidden springs where joy intertwines.

Unraveled Dreams Beneath Skin

Beneath the surface, where thoughts like to roam,
Are dreams tangled up like socks without a home.
The mind does somersaults, oh what a sight,
As hopes jiggle like jelly in the sweet moonlight.

A whisper of giggles hides in my chest,
While wishes take turns in a silly jest.
The heart throws a party, balloons in the air,
While worries conspire, but we just don't care.

With each unwound secret, a chuckle's released,
Like socks in the dryer, it's chaos unleashed.
A tangle of wishes and laughter combine,
In this riddle of life, each joke is divine.

So let's unravel the dreams that we keep,
And dance through the mess where our passions leap.
For in every twist, a new story begins,
Through the unraveled threads, our laughter wins.

Fragments of Light in Shadows

In a cupboard, dreams reside,
Where mismatched socks can hide.
A taco sings, a fish takes flight,
Potato chips glow in the night.

Whispers dance like fireflies,
While jellybeans wear silly ties.
The ceiling fan hums a tune,
As the cat declares it's noon.

Cupcakes tumble, sprinkles fly,
The blender shouts, oh me, oh my!
In every crevice, laughter peeks,
Like sneaky mice that play hide and seek.

Echoes of giggles fill the room,
With rubber chickens causing doom.
In light and shadows, secrets brawl,
Fragmented magic, after all.

The Garden of Uncharted Paths

In a garden, weeds take cheer,
They tell the daisies, 'Don't you fear!'
A snail races, the tortoise yawns,
Frilly blooms dance in their fawns.

Bugs throw parties, sipping dew,
While roses gossip about the view.
A pumpkin dreams to be a boat,
As daisies teach a goat to float.

Squirrels in capes save the day,
While radishes join in the fray.
In playful chaos, nature beams,
As broccoli plots its wacky schemes.

The moon peeks down to have a say,
In this garden where whims hold sway.
A topiary wizard waves his wand,
And all jokes land with a fond.

Moonlit Journeys Yet to Begin

Beneath the stars, a penguin flies,
With tiny wings and hopeful sighs.
He meets a cow that dances tall,
And serenades the moonlit all.

A llama in shades rides a bike,
Singing loudly, 'Hey, take a hike!'
With every pedal, laughter grows,
As marshmallows rain, and joy flows.

A road sign winks, 'This way to fun!'
While kangaroos hop, 'We've just begun!'
The compass spins, it can't decide,
Between ice cream and a wild slide.

In moonlit madness, dreams collide,
With every twist, let glee abide.
So pack your socks, let's take a ride,
Adventure awaits, open wide!

The Enigma of Lost Tomorrows

In a box of yesterdays, we find,
A sock with tales of time unkind.
Marbles roll like thoughts astray,
Chasing giggles, lost in play.

A clock melts like ice cream fun,
Time giggles, 'I will not run!'
Cacti wear sombreros bright,
As cactus plants join in the light.

A rubber duck speaks in rhyme,
Telling stories of lost time.
With a bubble wand, it declares,
"Every moment sings, who cares?"

Through maze of wonders, nonsense reigns,
With silly hats and phantom trains.
The enigma giggles, never borrows,
It's just a dance of lost tomorrows.

A Universe in My Palm

Tiny galaxies swirl,
In this hand I hold tight.
Stars bounce like rubber balls,
Cosmic giggles in flight.

Nebulas poke their heads,
From pockets of my jeans.
Comets with silly hats,
Dance in my wild dreams.

Journey Beyond the Ordinary

Off I go on a trip,
With socks that don't match up,
Finding butterflies that flip,
In the world's oversized cup.

Trains made of candy bars,
Ride tracks of licorice rope,
Sailing on chocolate cars,
Each bump a sugar dope.

The Treasure of Now

Here's a treasure map,
Marked with doodles and laughs,
X marks the happy nap,
Where sunlight makes me gaffes.

Golden moments glimmer,
Like fries in a warm breeze,
Catch them quick, don't shimmer,
Savor life's flavored tease.

Veils of Unwritten Stories

In my hat, a story waits,
Woven with giggling threads,
Every twist a funny fate,
Eagerly it gently spreads.

Dragons in crayon hues,
Whisper jokes in the night,
While owls wear silly shoes,
Turning fears into delight.

The Drama of Daring Choices

At the crossroads I stand, quite unsure,
Should I pick the right or sail down the blur?
One path leads to donuts, sweet and divine,
The other, a gym – oh, the laughter's mine!

Flip a coin or do the chicken dance,
Decisions abound; should I take a chance?
Friends cheer me on, some are in fits,
While I ponder my fate over nacho chips!

Will I dare to call it a daring quest?
Or just sit binge-watching – I must confess!
Each choice, a cliff on which I might trip,
Perhaps I'll just toss a fruit salad sip!

So here's to the whimsy of choices we make,
A dance with the joyous, a plunge in the lake!
With giggles, we navigate fun's winding path,
Daring each other to join in the laugh!

Stitches of Serendipity

Sewing my dreams with mismatched thread,
An odd decoration, or so it was said.
Noodles and daisies, what a wild style!
Each stitch a surprise, each moment a smile!

Found a sock with a hole? Make it a hat!
Transform your wardrobe, imagine that!
Spinning tales of blunders, we cheerily sew,
Who knew the fabric of life had this flow?

Accidental patterns, a quilt of pure glee,
Stitching together what's quirky in me.
With each little patch, a laugh blooms anew,
It's funny how friendship can cover the blue!

So raise up your needle, let laughter unite,
In stitches we gather, oh what a delight!
Life's a wild tapestry, rich with whimsy,
Sewn tight with adventure, let's get a little risky!

Voyage to the Possible

Pack your bags with socks and a snack,
We're voyaging to places that others lack!
Hop on the train of imagination's ride,
With a map drawn in crayons, what fun we'll decide!

The captain's a cat with a monocle on,
He'll steer us through laughter till the break of dawn.
We'll sail through the puddles where rainbows reside,
And dance with the jellybeans, come join the slide!

With compass of chuckles, we chart our own way,
Finding treasures of giggles that lead us astray.
Each island of whimsy, a new kind of thrill,
We'll dive in the bubbles, let joy be our will!

So grab a balloon, and let's take to the skies,
With balloons full of wishes and sparkly fries!
In this voyage of ruckus, together we'll sail,
Where fun is abundant and laughter won't fail!

Fragments of Forgotten Visions

A scribble on paper, a thought tossed away,
What happened to dreams that danced in my play?
A hat made of waffles, a shoe for my cat,
Let's gather these fragments, imagine that!

Once I thought I'd juggle with onions and cheese,
But all I achieved was a sandwich with ease.
Laughter erupts at those plans that we fail,
Those visions were treasures with giggle galore!!

A painting of splatters, all colors of joy,
I called it abstract, but just made a mess, oh boy!
Yet each silly moment a treasure to keep,
In the treasure chest of memories, we leap!

So let's celebrate mishaps, mistakes that we've made,
Each piece, a reminder of the fun we've played.
With giggles erupting and stories on hand,
Fragments of laughter make life truly grand!

Within the Fabric of Potential

In the corner of my coat, a button waits,
Like a treasure from a land of mates.
It whispers jokes of joy divine,
While hiding secrets made from twine.

A sock with holes, a quilt with flair,
Yes, there's magic hidden everywhere.
My mismatched shoes, they dance and spin,
Silly dreams that beckon me in.

A pen that draws on air so light,
Sketching wishes throughout the night.
The threads of laughter, stitched with care,
Creating chuckles in the air.

So here I am, with threads and seams,
Crafting castles from silly dreams.
Each little item, odd or neat,
Holds a journey beneath my feet.

The Canvas of What Could Be

A canvas bright with splashes wide,
Houses all the thoughts I hide.
A brush with sparkles, oh what fun,
Each stroke a giggle, just begun.

Crayons dance across the page,
With colors bold, they break the cage.
Imaginary friends all glee,
Painting worlds as bold as can be.

A splash of purple, a daub of green,
Every hue's a hidden scene.
I chuckle while my fingers glide,
Crafting tales I cannot hide.

So let the laughter take its flight,
As colors mingle, glow, and fight.
For on this canvas, wild and free,
Lie all the dreams that dare to be.

Seeds of Surrendered Ambition

Seeds I planted in my hat,
Hoping they would grow up fat.
A garden sprouting from my head,
With daisies dancing all instead.

Each one a wish, a funny prank,
Rooted deep in laughter's tank.
Sunshine giggles, rainbows sigh,
Who would know what grows up high?

Weeds appear, but who would care,
With silly blooms everywhere.
Chasing bugs with joyful screams,
Harvesting the best of dreams.

So here I stand, a farmer strange,
In a world where thoughts can change.
Surrendered dreams, so wild and free,
Blooming up in sheer jubilee.

Echoes of Bright Beginnings

At dawn, the sun, a silly grin,
Starts the day with a playful spin.
Banana peels on sidewalks lay,
As laughter takes a joyful sway.

With echoing giggles in the trees,
Whispers float with the lightest breeze.
From silly hats to dancing shoes,
Every moment is packed with cues.

A jump, a twirl, all hearts align,
Secret plans turn into wine.
So let's toast to all things bright,
Where beginnings spark and take their flight.

In this world of goofy starts,
Every echo speaks to hearts.
With each sunrise, let's not forget,
Life's a game without regret.

The Echoing Silence of Chances

In the closet of dreams, socks have a chat,
They whisper and giggle, imagine that!
A shoe tells a story of adventures gone wild,
While the dust bunnies dance, oh, how they smiled!

A key found in pocket, a lock with a grin,
'Try me,' it chuckles, 'let's see what's within!'
The clock hands are laughing, they tick-tock and play,
As ideas on paper just wander away!

A napkin with doodles, a treasure in ink,
Maps of imagination, they flow and they sink.
In the jar of the kitchen, a pickle's good cheer,
He giggles and wiggles, adventures are near!

So let's toss out a wish, let the laughter begin,
For chances like bubbles, they'll pop with a grin!
In the echo of silence, let whimsy resound,
In the place where the silly and sacred are found!

Fleeting Moments of Discovery

A sandwich that talks with jam for a voice,
Says, 'Pickle, come join me, let's make a good choice!'
The fridge hums a tune, off-key but so bold,
As leftovers argue, new stories unfold.

A cat with a secret, a hat on her head,
She claims she's the queen of the dreams that we've fed.
A sock that plays peek-a-boo under the bed,
Laughs when you trip, 'Who says I'm misled?'

In the garden, a gnome is stuck in his pose,
With daisies for pals and a toy dinosaur nose.
The wind sings a song, a whimsical jest,
As butterflies giggle and join in the fest!

So cherish those moments that flit like a bee,
In the foreground of life, it's absurdity's spree!
Each fleeting encounter, a chuckle to keep,
Like secrets in whispers that tickle our sleep!

Veins of Unseen Potential

Beneath the cold surface of an old garden hose,
A snake dreams of racing, yet no one knows.
A leaf on the ground does a jig with the breeze,
Saying, 'Watch me! I'm dancing! Just try to catch these!'

The shadows of sneakers make footprints of dreams,
They run and they leap as if bursting at seams.
A rock wants to travel, it claims it's a star,
But it's stuck in its spot, oh, how sad that they are!

The crayons are plotting, a masterpiece spree,
They'll color the world in absurd jubilee!
A coffee cup laughs as it's hugged, what a thrill,
It dreams of vacations and life at will!

So spot the potential in things small and round,
For magic is hiding where laughter is found.
In veins of the mundane, let joy always flow,
And feel all the wonders that life's whispers show!

Dreams Nestled in the Quiet

A pillow confesses, 'I cradle the dreams,
Of adventures at night under moonlit beams.'
A blanket, so cozy, begins to conspire,
Says, 'Shh, let's create our own campfire!'

In the stillness of dusk, the stars have a chat,
They wink at the moon, saying, 'Look at that!'
The dust on the shelf starts to dance on its own,
With the laughter of echoes, creation is sewn.

A coffee mug sighs, 'I brew up the fun,
With sips of imagination, let's start with one!'
The clock on the wall has a tickle fight,
While crickets compose the music of night.

So treasure the quiet, the moments that gleam,
For dreams in the stillness burst forth like a stream.
In the hush of the world, where oddities dwell,
Lies a treasure of laughter that chuckles so well!

The Promise of Tomorrow

In a box of laughter, dreams collide,
With silly hats and mismatched shoes wide.
Chasing bubbles that float in the air,
We trip on rubber ducks without a care.

A dance with shadows under the sun,
Banana peels make for a slippery run.
Tickling the future with a feather or two,
Who knew tomorrow could feel so askew?

With crayons drawing paths on the floor,
Imagined adventures behind every door.
Giggling at wonders, we bounce and sway,
The promise of laughs in every new day.

So come take my hand, let's leap with delight,
Embrace the absurd, take flight in the night.
In this wacky world, we'll make our stand,
With each goofy step, our fun is well planned.

Cradle of Infinite Paths

In a land where whimsy reigns supreme,
Lost socks become boats in the river of dreams.
We chase our tails in a lively parade,
Finding treasure in every odd jigsaw laid.

A chicken in shoes asks for a dance,
The kazoo serenades with a joyful chance.
With each little giggle and whimsical cheer,
The cradle of paths spins far and near.

Shadows of silliness twirl in the night,
With jellybean stars that shine oh so bright.
Sprinting through puddles, splashes galore,
Every step taken invites us for more.

So gather your friends for a colorful spree,
In a world where the silly is wild and free.
With laughter as currency, we trade with glee,
In this cradle of paths, just come and see!

Unfolding Wishes

In a garden of dreams, where wishes take flight,
We sprout silly hats made of pure moonlight.
Unicorns giggle while painting the sky,
As marbles roll on, watching time fly by.

With each folded paper, a new tale begins,
Kites made of laughter bring joy as it spins.
The sun plays peek-a-boo behind fluffy clouds,
While we jump in puddles, loud and proud.

Whispers of wishes that wiggle and dance,
Acrobatic dreams that leap at a chance.
Bubblegum rainbows sweep through the night,
As we map our future with crayons and light.

So come, let's twirl in this magical place,
Where silliness blossoms with every embrace.
With unfolded wishes that twinkle and gleam,
We paint our own stories, a vibrant dream.

Tides of Unseen Horizons

On shores where sandcastles face the tide,
We ride waves of giggles with glee as our guide.
Shells whisper secrets of the ludicrous past,
In this land of laughter, let's make memories vast.

With jellyfish dancing beneath the moonlight,
And rubber ducks racing with pure delight.
The ocean waves wiggle, tickle our toes,
As we chase after rainbows where the sea breeze blows.

Tides rolling in, bringing silliness anew,
A surfboard of dreams glides where the fun grew.
With each little splash, we giggle and cheer,
In the dance of horizons, we banish all fear.

So grab your floatie, let's drift and explore,
In this whimsical world, we can't help but adore.
With laughter as our compass, we'll sail far and bright,
Into tides of unseen horizons, pure delight.

Wonders in the Weaving

In a sock, a mouse resides,
With mismatched shoes, he takes great strides.
He twirls around on rainy days,
While sunbeams dance in playful ways.

His hat is made of chewed-up gum,
And every step sounds like a drum.
He climbs the curtain, swings on a thread,
Just don't tell mom; stay under the bed!

A cheese parade is on the way,
With little feet that come to play.
They play hopscotch on the floor,
While sneaky cats sneak out the door!

In this house of wild delight,
Where socks can dream and shadows bite.
Each giggle's worth a thousand suns,
In this weird world of stolen funs.

Opportunities in the Shadows

In the nooks where shadows cling,
Little sprights with tiny wings,
They plan a feast of jellybeans,
To lure the grumpy, warty queens.

Under beds, they toss confetti,
Bringing fun when days are sweaty.
They mix up soup with crayons bright,
And dance along with pure delight.

A mailbox opens wide for mail,
Inviting giggles, not a wail.
A letter writes itself today,
'Come, let's play! Hip Hip Hooray!'

In dim places where laughter hides,
Life appears in silly strides.
With bubbling joy in every peek,
Opposites become the seek-and-squeak.

Threads of Wandering Whimsy

On a bike made out of cheese,
Pedaling fast with squeaky knees.
This little dreamer flies so high,
With patchwork wings, he dares the sky.

With lollipops that taste like rain,
He takes a stroll on candy cane.
The clouds are marshmallow fluff,
And he insists that's quite enough.

A raccoon wears a dapper hat,
And claims it's best; just look at that!
He juggles pinecones one by one,
As sassy squirrels cheer for fun.

Across the fields, the zephyr calls,
Through cotton candy, laughter sprawls.
With every step, an adventure blooms,
In fabrics thick with giggles' rooms.

Light in the Unexplored

In a cellar, strange things wiggle,
A fish in boots begins to giggle.
With neon lights and jumping jacks,
They spin around, avoiding snacks.

A treasure map that leads to snacks,
With licorice trails and chatty quacks.
They plot to find the soda spring,
And bounce around like crazy bling.

In this nook, the oddities play,
As jars of jelly come out to sway.
Each unturned stone reveals a laugh,
And giggly plans found in a gaffe.

Light filters through in vivid hues,
As broomsticks dance, as if they choose.
A kingdom built on sweets and spritz,
In the unexplored, life truly flits.

The Uncharted Voyage

We set sail on a rubber duck,
With maps made of candy and pure luck,
The compass points toward a giant pie,
But somehow we just float on by.

Each wave a giggle, each breeze a cheer,
With seagulls yelling, "What's over here?"
The ocean's a giant bowl of soup,
And here we are, just sipping from the scoop.

Mermaids dance in flip-flops and shades,
While jellyfish offer us lemonade,
We whirl through islands of whipped cream delight,
So grab your spoon, let's dine tonight!

But wait, what's this? A treasure of socks,
All mismatched patterns, with silly clocks,
Our voyage ends, but it begins anew,
In a world where fun wears something askew.

Flickers of Dreamed Identities

I wake as a llama in a tuxedo fine,
With a monocle perched, I sip some wine,
At a party of zebras who dance with flair,
Oops! I stepped on a giraffe's long hair!

Every mirror's cracked in this silly realm,
Where chickens rule and penguins helm,
I mingle with hippos in glittery hats,
While squirrels recite Shakespeare to chitchat.

A disco ball spins, it's quite the sight,
With raccoons breakdancing under the light,
I shout, "To be fabulous is the real quest!"
As the flamingos take a glitter-bombed rest.

Tomorrow I'll wake as a three-headed cat,
Each one with quirks, the tallest quite fat,
In dreams like these, the fun never ends,
Flickers of laughter in hues that transcend.

Layers of Unseen Futures

Beneath my bed, a portal lies,
It leads to a land of floating pies,
Where every tree grows candy canes,
And laughter dances on joyfully rains.

I wear a hat made of fruit cocktails,
With birds that tell the funniest tales,
Each step I take plants a new idea,
Like a talking chair that plays a banjo's cheer!

The time is now to create your fate,
With talking clocks that can't be late,
I'll be a chef, a knight, or a whale,
In layers of dreams, where laughter prevails.

The future's a dance, a giggly waltz,
With gumball stars and folks without faults,
Let's peel back the layers and take the ride,
Into a world where weirdness is our guide.

Roadmaps to the Unimagined

In my backpack's a map of dreams,
With directions marked by silly schemes,
To find the land of the wibbly-wobble,
Where ideas bounce and laughter gobbles.

Follow the path lined with purple trees,
And suddenly, talking fish join the breeze,
The clouds are made of marshmallow fluff,
On this journey, there's never enough!

A merely normal rock says, "Who's that?"
While busy bees chatter, wearing a hat,
We're off to explore, with cheer in our toes,
No destination's fixed, just where laughter flows.

At the end of the road is a giant cake,
But wait! That's not all that's at stake,
With every step, new dreams will appear,
In the land of the unimagined, let's cheer!

Navigating the Crossroads of Fate

At the fork, I saw two paths,
One lined with cake, the other with baths.
I weighed my options, took a glance,
Then slipped on a banana peel right in advance.

Why do the signs all point to pizza?
A slice in hand, I'm a true believer.
With a map that's scribbled and a compass that's bent,
I'm lost in laughter but I'm not in dissent.

A squirrel asked for directions, so I obliged,
He pointed me towards the path of fried pies.
With every choice, my shoes are untied,
But who cares when you've got a dance party inside?

So here's to the journey, wherever it leads,
Life's a comedy sketch planted with seeds.
At each intersection, I hear fate's soft laugh,
Guiding me safely to the joke of the path.

Reflections in Quiet Waters

I peered into the lake, my face was a mess,
A duck quacked at me, what did I possess?
The ripples giggled, the frogs stood to cheer,
As I waved to my reflection—was that really me here?

The fish wore bow ties, the turtles wore hats,
All having tea with the chattiest rats.
With a splash of the oar and a flip of the wrist,
I joined in their party, couldn't resist!

As the sun set low, I tried to jump in,
But tripped over lily pads, oh where to begin?
With laughter echoing over the mirror-like pond,
I sent a few ripples, my worries were gone.

So here in this moment of chuckles and splashes,
Nature's a clown, through all of life's thrashes.
Reflections might waver, and that's quite alright,
For the silliest memories bring pure delight.

The Birth of New Beginnings

I woke up this morning with a spring in my shoe,
Today's the day! A whole world to pursue.
But first, I spilled coffee, it flew through the room,
Now my cat's plotting how to escape the gloom.

With my hands smeared brown and no time to spare,
I leaped out the door, though almost lost a hair.
Every new step, a curious flop,
Discoveries await, oh what a nonstop!

At the corner I startled a pigeon or two,
As they flapped in panic, I waved them adieu.
Found a hot dog stand, with relish galore,
But the sauce took a trip… now it's out for more!

In each little mishap, a chance to invent,
From ruckus and chaos, my moments are spent.
So here's to the start and all that it brings,
Embrace every oops, and see what it sings!

Rays of Hope in the Mundane

Woke up with a sock stuck tight on my head,
Thought I'd rock the look, like a fashion thread.
With toast in one hand and a shoe on my foot,
I danced to the bathroom—so silly, yet cute!

The world may seem dull, like leftovers reheat,
But I'll twirl like a chef, flip my frown with a feat.
Found a lost penny—my lucky charm,
Now I'm off to make mayhem, and raise some alarm!

The laundry's a monster, it's eating my clothes,
A sock puppet war is just how this goes.
With mismatched patterns and colors gone wild,
I found joy in the chaos—call me a child!

So here in the mundane, with laughter and cheer,
Every moment's a gift, let's raise up a beer!
For life's not just routine, it's a cosmic parade,
And I'll march with a smile, unafraid and unmade.

Adventures in Invisibility

Invisibility cloaks, oh what a treat,
Wearing one feels like a sneaky feat.
I tiptoe past folks, with giggles so bright,
Hands waving but no one gives me a fright.

I drop a soft potato, it rolls on by,
Neighbors just stare, and I can't help but cry.
With each little blunder, I chuckle and grin,
Invisible pranks, where will they begin?

I painted my cat in stripes of pure green,
Now she's the swirl in my wild-daydream scene.
She pounces through silence, a ghost in the night,
Chasing her tail like a star taking flight.

Oh, the joy of this cloak, the giggles it yields,
In a world where my antics are shielded, concealed.
I'll invite all my friends, we'll dance in the dusk,
In the cloak of invisibility, oh what a husk!

The Symphony of Unexpected Paths

There once was a road that twisted and turned,
With mismatched directions, my head yearned.
I chose a left when I should've gone right,
And found a fine jazz band playing all night.

The trombone was played by a dog on the chase,
While cats played the drums with impeccable grace.
I danced with my shoes all tied up in a knot,
Adventurous spirits, we danced on the spot.

The notes flew like butterflies, wild and so free,
We twirled in the chaos, just you wait and see.
Every blunder was music, a laugh in the air,
In this symphony of life, not a single care.

So follow the twists, laughter's the key,
Unexpected paths may lead you to glee.
Embrace every wrong turn, for what could go wrong?
Just join in the chorus, let's sing our new song!

Inkblots of New Realities

A splash of ink here, a blot over there,
Creating new worlds with colors to share.
I see a cat wearing a fanciful hat,
Next to a mouse that's dancing on chat.

In this whimsical mess, a world starts to form,
Where umbrellas bloom and rainbows keep warm.
A sandwich sails by with a smile on its face,
Adding a sprinkle of quirk to this place.

My pen trips and slides, but oh what a thrill,
As mountains grow legs and begin to fulfill.
They dance with the clouds, as giggles ensue,
Bringing to life what only ink can do.

So grab a blue pen, make art as you go,
Inkblots of laughter will steal the show.
What links wacky visuals, twisty and bright,
Is the joy of each scribble, a pure delight!

The Secret Garden of Dreams

In a garden, so secret, where giggles grow wild,
A unicorn skates while the flowers get styled.
They wear funky glasses and bowties with flair,
While critters with top hats prance everywhere.

A snail sips hot cocoa, relaxing so slow,
While hedgehogs in robes trade their secrets, you know.
Each petal a whisper, each leaf holds a joke,
In this merry place, where nonsense awoke.

A rainbow-skin butterfly graces the air,
With jokes on the wind, laughter's everywhere.
Nearby, a sweet fountain spills giggles galore,
As friends from the forest play games on the floor.

So wander the path with a grin on your face,
In this secret garden, it's a whimsical space.
Where dreams are all goofy and laughter's the theme,
You'll find joy blooming in every bright beam!

Exploring the Labyrinth of Dreams

In dreams, I wander with a grin,
Chasing shadows, eager to win.
A talking cat offers me a shoe,
"Wear it, mate, and let's rendezvous!"

I stumble on clouds, trip over stars,
Chat with Martians from afar.
They pay me in jellybeans and cheer,
"Stay for a while! Don't show fear!"

The walls are made of marshmallow fluff,
I bounce and laugh; it's all just stuff.
A quirky gnome plays on a sax,
And I can't help but dance with facts!

With whimsy wrapped around my head,
I toss my worries, not a shred.
In this maze of mirth, I'll forever roam,
For laughter echoes; this is my home!

Sculpting Possibility from the Void

In the void, I mold with laughter,
Shaping dreams, a spirited crafter.
Balloon animals twist in the dark,
They giggle and prance in a delightful arc.

I sculpt a unicorn from pure jest,
Whose mane is made of that silly zest.
It sneezes glitter into the air,
And suddenly, joy is everywhere!

Stars come alive for the performance,
Juggling planets with endless endurance.
Cosmic ketchup spills on the floor,
Spaghetti chaos—who could ask for more?

In this creation of boundless cheer,
I mold the goofy, it's perfectly clear.
With every twist the void takes form,
Laughter's the magic, my heart to warm!

The Horizon of Unexplored Visions

On the horizon, strange sights appear,
A disco ball spins; I cannot steer.
Riding a whale with polka dot bliss,
I take a tumble but can't resist!

Fortune cookies flutter like flies,
Spitting wisdom in wacky ties.
"Dance like no one's watching!" they say,
And I twirl 'round, laughing all the way.

A hot air balloon made of cereal,
Carries me high; it's a big deal!
With marshmallow clouds and soda streams,
Reality bends, it bursts at the seams.

Though I may wobble and sway at times,
I chase these visions with upbeat rhymes.
The horizon giggles, a wondrous sight,
With every sunset, it's pure delight!

A Glimpse Beyond the Veil

Peeking past where the wild things roam,
There's a garden gnome in a stylish chrome.
He shows me wonders, a circus parade,
With juggling frogs and a funky charade.

A ghost on a skateboard zips on by,
"Try this trick!" with a laugh and a sigh.
As I tumble headfirst—oh, what a sight!
A twist of fate, and it feels just right.

Beyond the veil, where giggles abound,
Silly creatures frolic without a sound.
They dip and dive in puddles of glee,
A symphony formed, just wait and see!

With each epic fail and funny surprise,
I discover that joy is the brightest prize.
So I'll peek through this veil, *why not*, I say,
For laughter is magic that brightens the day!

The Dance of Maybes

In a world where dreams take flight,
I jitterbug with could-be's at night.
Twirl with whimsies, spin with glee,
Maybe I'll be a bird, or a tree!

Here's a waltz for every whim,
A half-hearted hop, a raucous rim.
Frolicking with wishes, all a tease,
What if I'm a jester, just to please?

I sashay in slippers, one left, one right,
Embracing the odd, oh what a sight!
The moon laughs softly; it's all a blip,
As I discover new moves on this trip.

With giggles as music, this floor is vast,
Every choice echoes; good times are cast.
So, join me now in this whimsical spree,
The dance of maybes, wild and free!

Notes from the Edge of Eternity

On the brink where whispers play,
I scribble my hopes like kids with clay.
Each thought a note in a cosmic song,
Jumbled tunes where we all belong.

Gravity laughs as I send dreams ahead,
While scribbling wishes on a slice of bread.
I toss notes to the stars with giddy flair,
Laughter erupts from the cosmic air.

In margins of time, I doodle and draw,
Chasing the echoes like I'm in a law.
Tick-tock goes the clock with a wink,
In the edge of forever, let's laugh and think!

So grab your quill, let's write our fate,
With whimsy and mischief, let's celebrate!
Here at the brink, with giggles and glee,
We craft our legacies, wild and free!

The Waiting Room of Aspirations

In the lobby of hopes, we sit in line,
With dreams in our pocket, all divine.
An old clock ticks with a smirking face,
As we tap our feet, dreaming of grace.

Magazines rustle with tales of stars,
They whisper of journeys that'll take us far.
Yet we're stuck here with sandwiches and tea,
Is this the start? Or just a spree?

"Next!" calls a voice, it's time to go!
But hold on tight, let the laughter flow.
For every moment spent, a jest awaits,
While we spin tales of whimsical fates.

So let's lounge on chairs, where the silly reigns,
Where waiting for dreams is all in the chains.
In this room of hopes, let's savor the ride,
For laughter's the key, where aspirations abide!

Roads Less Traveled in Midnight

At midnight's hour, I map my paths,
With streetlights winking and shadowed laughs.
Each turn a riddle, where giggles ensue,
With mischief brewing, just me and you.

The moon rides along, a jester in light,
Lighting the way for a playful night.
Every intersection whispers a jest,
As we wander down roads that are truly blessed.

Why take the straight when curves are a blast?
Here's to silly detours and fun unsurpassed.
Laughter echoes in each hidden nook,
As we tread the path, not found in a book.

So grab my hand, let's dance on the street,
With twirls and spins, feel the thrill and beat.
For in the dark, under stars so bright,
The roads less traveled are pure delight!

www.ingramcontent.com/pod-product-compliance
Lightning Source LLC
Chambersburg PA
CBHW070316120526
44590CB00017B/2703